THE BIBLE CURE®

FOR

STRESS

D0974350

DON COLBERT, M.D.

SILOAM PRESS

Living in Health—Body, Mind and Spirit

THE BIBLE CURE FOR STRESS
by Don Colbert, M.D.
Published by Siloam Press
A part of Strang Communications Company
600 Rinehart Road
Lake Mary, Florida 32746
www.siloampress.com

Scripture quotations marked NIV are from the Holy Bible, New International Version. Copyright © 1973, 1978, 1984, International Bible Society. Used by permission.

Library of Congress Cataloging-in-Publication Data:
2002101778
International Standard Book Number: 0-88419-826-X

This book is not intended to provide medical advice or to take the place of medical advice and treatment from your personal physician. Readers are advised to consult their own doctors or other qualified health professionals regarding the treatment of their medical problems. Neither the publisher nor the author takes any responsibility for any possible consequences from any treatment, action or application of medicine, supplement, herb or preparation to any person reading or following the information in this book. If readers are taking prescription medications, they should consult with their physicians and not take themselves off of medicines to start supplementation without the proper supervision of a physician.

02 03 04 05 06   9876543
Printed in the United States of America

Feeling
Stressed Out?

You may be living in one of the most stressful times in recent history. Daily you are being forced to cope with an onslaught of political fear and insecurity, financial uncertainty, constantly increasing job demands, relationship pressures and much, much more. If stress is making you feel like a kettle that's reached its boiling point, then you've come to the right place. There is hope for you! You really can conquer stress and its overwhelming mental and physical effects.

By picking up this Bible Cure booklet, you have taken an exciting first step toward successfully surviving and conquering stress and reclaiming control over your spiritual, emotional and physical health. Right now you may be confronting some of the greatest challenges of your life. But by understanding some of the "real" root causes of your stressed-out feelings, you can rise to a new level of physical, emotional and spiritual health and joy in God.

God revealed His divine will for each of us through the apostle John, who wrote, "Dear friend, I am praying that all is well with you and that *your body is as healthy as I know your soul is*" (3 John 2, emphasis added). Surely when we are stressed out we are missing God's best for us. But how? A closer look will reveal some hopeful answers.

Addressing the Spiritual Roots of Disease

As a Christian medical doctor I've studied and prayed about the causes of disease, and increasingly I've discovered that many diseases have very strong spiritual roots. If you are familiar with my books, then doubtless you are aware that I believe in the health of the entire person: body, mind and spirit. Although traditional medicine often sees these facets of our being as very separate, in truth they are not. A vital link exists between the spirit, soul and body. And although much of the disease and physical pain we suffer comes from the body, often these distresses begin in the soul, which encompasses the mind and emotions.

Therefore, truly walking in the divine health that God intends for us requires that we look a little deeper, beyond the physical process of disease to the spiritual, emotional and mental roots. I trust that you will find these pages extremely enlightening as you gain new insight and revelation to help you live your life in the robust, joyful state of good health that God desires for you.

Stress and Your Health

Surveys and research over the past two decades reveal these startling statistics concerning stress:

- Forty-three percent of all adults suffer adverse health effects due to stress.
- Seventy-five to 90 percent of all visits to primary care physicians are for stress-related complaints or disorders.
- Chronic stress has been linked to most of the leading causes of death, including heart disease, cancer, lung ailments, accidents, cirrhosis and suicide.
- On an average workday an estimated one million workers are absent because of stress-related complaints. Stress is said to be responsible for more than half of the

550,000,000 workdays lost annually because of absenteeism.

- A three-year study conducted by a large corporation showed that 60 percent of employee absences were due to psychological problems such as stress.[1]

Today, the negative results of stress are at an all-time high. But you do not have to sit back and become one more stress statistic. With God's help, you can fight back and win. So, as you begin to read through the pages of this booklet, get ready to feel better!

This Bible Cure booklet is filled with hope and encouragement for understanding how to keep your body fit and healthy. In this book, you will

> *uncover God's divine plan of health*
> *for body, soul and spirit*
> *through modern medicine,*
> *good nutrition,*
> *and the medicinal power*
> *of Scripture and prayer.*

You will find key scripture passages throughout this book that will help you focus on the power of God. These divine promises will empower your prayers and redirect your thoughts to line up with God's plan of divine health for you—a plan that includes victory over stress and its destructive physical and emotional effects.

In this Bible Cure booklet, you will learn how to subdue stress as you study the following chapters:

There is much you can do to rise above stress and its negative health impact upon your life. You really can stand up and face the challenges of stress with fresh confidence, renewed determination and the wonderful knowledge that God is real, that He is alive and that His power is greater than any other force in the universe.

It is my prayer that these powerful strategies for conquering stress will bring health, wholeness and spiritual refreshing to you—body, mind and spirit. May they deepen your fellowship with God and strengthen your ability to worship and serve Him.

—DON COLBERT, M.D.

A BIBLE CURE PRAYER
FOR YOU

Dear heavenly Father, You created me, and You are well aware of the pressures and emotional turmoil that surround me every day. As I read through this Bible Cure booklet, give me a special grace to rise up to a bold new level of faith and courage in You.

God, I thank You that before my circumstances were ever set in motion, You had created a plan for my victory over them. Thank You for Your wonderful Word, which promises special protection and deliverance when I am tempted to feel overwhelmed by stressful circumstances. Thank You for making it possible for me to walk in Your divine health for my total being—body, mind and spirit—free from the physical and emotional ravages of stress. In Jesus' name, amen.

Chapter 1

Understanding the Roots of Stress

The Bible says, "People judge by outward appearance, but the LORD looks at a person's thoughts and intentions" (1 Sam. 16:7). In other words, God looks far beyond what people see, for He is able to see the very root of a problem.

Often I meet people who complain about the modern medical profession. They tell me that their doctors seem to merely treat symptoms with a variety of chemicals and drugs, but seldom do they attempt to discover the root causes. Under the present medical system in America, today's physicians often can be left feeling like little more than legal drug dispensers.

God promises us that if we seek, we will find. If we knock, the door will open to us. (See Luke

11:9.) He promises to give us wisdom and understanding; all we must do is ask Him for it. To understand and overcome stress, I believe it is extremely important to go beyond simple chemical remedies, such as Prozac, that merely mask the symptoms.

What would happen if the red oil light in your car was on and you took it to a mechanic to have the warning light turned off? The annoying problem has been alleviated, but the root could remain. In time, the problem would grow much worse, creating even more serious symptoms. Before long, your engine could be destroyed because you only treated the symptoms and never discovered the root cause.

> *So I advise you to live according to your new life in the Holy Spirit. Then you won't be doing what your sinful nature craves.*
> —GALATIANS 5:16

Your body is much the same. Stress is little more than a symptom of something much more serious lying right beneath the surface of your life. If you don't discover the root of your stress, eventually you could end up in disaster.

So, let's dig a little deeper to begin to understand how stressed out you really are.

What Is Stress?

The dictionary defines *stress* as "mental or physical tension or strain." Stress involves the pressures of life and how you perceive, believe, react and cope with those pressures.

We have mentioned that chronic stress has been linked to many diseases, including heart disease, high blood pressure, spastic colon, tension headaches, ulcers, cancer, chronic fatigue, insomnia, depression, anxiety, strokes, asthma, skin rashes, increased heart rate, panic attacks and much more.

Stressful feelings are very often the result of:

- The demands placed upon us by everyday life.
- The major lifestyle changes with which we must deal.

One of the most stressful life events you can face is the loss of employment. If recently you've lost a job or know someone who has, then you are well aware of the stress involved. In times of financial uncertainty, learning a strategy to help you cope with stress can be a lifesaver. Read on for some powerful information that can get you through this challenging period of time.

A Life-Event Test

Take this life-event test to determine how the changes in your lifestyle affect your stress levels as compared to others. You may be surprised to discover how much your lifestyle changes have affected the levels of stress in your life.

____	Death of a spouse (or child)	100
____	Divorce	73
____	Marital separation	65
____	Jail term	63
____	Death of close family member	63
____	Personal injury or illness	53
____	Marriage	50
____	Fired at work	47
____	Marital reconciliation	45
____	Retirement	45
____	Change in family member's health	44
____	Pregnancy	40
____	Sex difficulties	39
____	Addition to family	39
____	Business readjustment	39
____	Change in financial state	38
____	Death of close friend	37
____	Change to different line of work	36
____	Change in number of marital arguments	35

___	Mortgage or loan for major purchases	31
___	Foreclosure of mortgage or loan	30
___	Change in work responsibilities	29
___	Son or daughter leaving home	29
___	Trouble with in-laws	29
___	Outstanding personal achievement	28
___	Spouse begins or stops work	26
___	Starting or finishing school	26
___	Change in living conditions	25
___	Revision of personal habits	24
___	Trouble with boss	23
___	Change in work hours, conditions	20
___	Change in residence	20
___	Change in schools	20
___	Change in recreational habits	19
___	Change in church activities	19
___	Change in social activities	18
___	Loan for minor purchase (car, TV, etc.)	17
___	Change in sleeping habits	16
___	Change in number of family gatherings	15
___	Change in eating habits	15
___	Vacation	13
___	Christmas season	12
___	Minor violations of the law	11
Total score		___

Now, add up the point values of all the items you checked. If your score is 300 or more, according to statistics you stand an almost 80 percent chance of getting sick in the near future. If your score is 150 to 299, your chances of becoming ill are about 50 percent. If less than 150, your chance of illness is about 30 percent.

Lifestyle change requires first an effort to adjust to the change, followed by an effort to regain stability. This self-evaluation suggests that significant change in your lifestyle saps energy from the body that it would ordinarily use to maintain itself, so reserves of energy are depleted and susceptibility to illness increases.

How Did You Score?

Well, how did you score? Do you have more stress-producing life events than you might have guessed? Even if your score was lower than you anticipated, your score does not necessarily indicate how YOU, as an individual, feel and react to stress. Stress is a very individualistic experience.

How You React

Not everyone reacts to the same circumstances by feeling the same degree of stress. One person might go skydiving for fun and relaxation, while for another this experience would feel like the most stressful time of his or her life. Since one person's stress can be another person's vacation, we see that stress is a result of how we as individuals interpret the events in our world. We cannot always control the many stressful circumstances that surround our lives, but we can control our reactions to those events. Understanding how to deal with the root causes of stress is a vital key to managing stress. We'll investigate this further later on in this little booklet.

Good vs. Bad Stress—
Too Much vs. Too Little

It may surprise you to learn that not all stress is bad. In fact, some stress is very beneficial. What determines whether it's good or bad is *how much* stress you are under. A little stress can be good, and too much stress can be very bad.

Stress is similar to the tuning of guitar strings. Just the right amount of pressure on the tuning peg of the guitar is required to gain the desired sound. But when you pull the

> *You will keep in perfect peace all who trust in you, whose thoughts are fixed on you!*
> —Isaiah 26:3

7

string too tightly, it can break when played, and the musical sound will stop.

In the same way, too much stress in your life can cause you to perform poorly, creating anxiety, nervousness, depression, irritability, forgetfulness, problems concentrating and problems making decisions. This happens when the pressures of life exceed your ability to cope. This "bad" stress is little more than "dis-stress," or the hopelessness and helplessness that come with feeling you've lost control over your circumstances. Distress makes you wonder whether or not to simply give up.

> *Because of God's tender mercy, the light from heaven is about to break upon us, to give light to those who sit in darkness and in the shadow of death, and to guide us to the path of peace.*
> —LUKE 1:78–79

Too little stress on that guitar string also creates a negative effect. Without some tension on the strings, the music sounds horrible. Similarly, too little stress in your life can leave you feeling bored, restless, understimulated and unable to perform adequately.

Therefore, the problem of stress is not the stress itself. The problem is not understanding yourself, your body, your health and your lifestyle well enough to allow the right amount of stress—the perfect tension for those guitar strings—so that your mind and body produce the good music of physical, mental and spiritual harmony.

So, let's see what stress looks like at the physical level. What happens in your body during moments of stress?

Understanding Stress

Dr. Hans Selye, who is known as the father of stress research, experimented with rats using many different physical events that created stress, such as electrical shocks and very cold temperatures. By doing this, Dr. Selye determined that when stress is maintained long enough, the body undergoes three distinctly different stages. He called these stages:

- The alarm stage
- The resistance stage
- The exhaustion stage

We're going to look closely at these three different stress stages. Take note of your own stress symptoms, and see if you can determine the stage of stress you may be experiencing.

Stage 1—The Alarm Stage

The alarm stage is the fight-or-flight emergency alarm system that God created in your body for survival. In the case of your ancestors, this protective system would have gone into action when your great-grandfather found himself trapped by a bear as he hunted in the woods.

He turns around, and there it is—a giant grizzly that is as mad as an angry hornet over being disturbed. Now, in the alarm stage, high-powered, potent chemicals that God has placed within us begin to circulate in your great-grandfather. Here is what happens physically:

Don't copy the behavior and customs of this world, but let God transform you into a new person by changing the way you think.
—ROMANS 12:2

A red light and an ear-deafening siren go off in the hypothalamus, an area in the brain. Now the brain is on red alert; therefore, it sends a signal to the pituitary gland to release a hormone that activates the adrenal glands.

Adrenaline (or epinephrine), a hormone that is released from the emergency alert adrenal glands located just above the kidneys, races through the body, sending it into high alert. The brain becomes very focused, eyesight sharpens and muscles tense as they prepare for fighting or fleeing. Heart rate and blood pressure increase as blood vessels constrict.

Primed for the Fight

Your great-grandfather's heart is pounding, his breathing becomes faster and deeper, and his blood sugar rises to supply fuel for the muscles.

This alarm stage of stress sets in motion a release of fats—an emergency fuel supply. Triglycerides, which are fats, race through the bloodstream. These fats as well as sugars fuel the muscles for fighting or fleeing. Blood is shunted away from the stomach and intestines—there's no time for digesting food, and besides, the body needs this extra blood to be pumped to the muscles to enable it to attack or run.

In this state, the digestive tract shuts down or at least functions at a far diminished capacity. The secretion of saliva slows down as well—your great-grandfather's mouth is feeling as dry as sagebrush.

The thyroid is stimulated, too, increasing the metabolic rate as it kicks out thyroid hormone. Blood is able to clot faster, which could save your great-grandfather's life if he were viciously attacked.

Now the great grizzly is getting ready to sink its giant teeth right in your great-grandfather's face. Just as your great-grandfather gets ready to react, the mammoth grizzly hears a loud noise from out of the woods. One of its cubs has fallen through some branches and is screaming for help. As the monster bear gives a final terrifying growl through its nasty yellow teeth and turns around, lumbering quickly away, your great-grandfather falls backward in relief. By the time he gets back to his log cabin, his stress reaction has nearly returned to normal. By morning, his body's hormonal system will function as though the event never happened.

What an incredible creation our bodies are! This amazing alarm system provided what pioneers needed to face the challenges of wagon trains, wild animal attacks and prairie fires.

Immersed in the amazing tranquility of God's creation, the body would quickly return to a healthy, normally functioning state.

Stress Beyond the Prairie

That was over a century ago, and life has changed

a great deal since then.

The stressors that threaten us don't come as an occasional, terrifying wild animal attack. Today's stresses come to us in the form of deadlines at work, financial pressures, traffic jams, political assaults that we witness each evening on the television news and ongoing random acts of terror from hidden sources.

The physical response of your great-grandfather's body during his encounter with the bear may happen to your body ten, twenty, thirty or even a hundred times daily due to the stresses of modern life. Today's psychological and emotional stress is far more constant and continuous than an occasional prairie fire or wild animal attack.

Because of this constant nature of modern-day stress, our bodies are not able to dissipate the stress chemicals as our ancestor's could. Stress chemicals continuously flood into our systems, preparing our bodies to either fight or flee. But many of us can only fume as we sit stranded in traffic with nothing to do while these chemicals race through our bodies raising our blood pressure, increasing our blood sugar, increasing our cholesterol, increasing our fats, raising cortisol levels and slowly causing our bones to melt away. Therefore, we end up literally stewing in our own juices.

Our bodies are being bombarded with powerful stress chemicals with no outlet because we are constantly undergoing powerful stress responses for seemingly frivolous reasons. Stress chemicals are being released driving to work, in disagreements with fellow employees, in battles with a spouse, in rebellion wars with teenagers and as we participate in the political and financial turmoil of modern times.

God designed this emergency alarm system to be used to save our lives by fleeing or fighting. Instead, these stress chemicals are being triggered in our bodies hundreds of times a day, and as a result, chronic, degenerative diseases are killing Americans at earlier and earlier ages. The Bible tells us that men's hearts will fail them for fear in the last days. (See Luke 21:26.) This is happening right now!

> *Casting down imaginations, and every high thing that exalteth itself against the knowledge of God, and bringing into captivity every thought to the obedience of Christ.*
> —2 CORINTHIANS 10:5, KJV

Stage 2—The Resistance Stage

As we mentioned, the number of individuals visiting doctors' offices for stress-related disorders is at an all-time high. As I see patients, I've noticed that some come when they are suffering only from the alarm stage of stress. But the great majority of stressed-out individuals I see are suffering the later resistance or exhaustion stages of stress. The chances are that if you have been dealing with too much stress for a prolonged time, you may be among that majority.

Let's look at the progression of these dangerous stress levels as they move into the second stage: the *resistance stage.*

When your body's emergency alarm response becomes more frequent, or if you feel that you have lost control, you are a candidate for the *resistance stage* of stress. This stage can kick in, for example, with an extended time of unemployment, a chronic illness, long-standing marital problems, the grief of having a child on drugs, a long-term financial crisis or any other negative circumstances that produce an ongoing feeling of hopelessness and helplessness.

When your body enters the resistance stage of stress, it continually pumps powerful chemicals into your bloodstream, including the highly charged hormones *cortisol* and *adrenaline.*

As we saw in great-grandfather's emergency, the hypothalamus becomes stimulated. It, in turn, stimulates the pituitary gland to release the hormone that activates the adrenal glands. These little glands that sit above the kidneys manufacture cortisol and adrenaline and furiously pump them into your body. In stage 2, elevated levels of both cortisol and adrenaline are usually present.

Commander Cortisol

Cortisol is a stress hormone that God placed within each of us to help sustain us during a prolonged crisis. During months of disease or other difficult circumstances of protracted stress, this powerful hormone can save your life. However, when you are continually living and working under significant levels of stress so that you begin to believe that there's no way out, here's what can happen.

Diabetes

A prolonged release of cortisol can lead to significantly elevated blood sugar levels. In the alarm stage, these hormones are released and blood sugar levels become elevated for a short duration of time and then return to normal. But when cortisol levels become chronically elevated, then your blood sugar may begin to rise, leading to increased insulin levels. Over time, this may lead to diabetes as insulin receptors become resistant to insulin.

Triglycerides, which are released into your bloodstream as fuel, may also stay elevated. High levels of triglycerides are associated with elevated cholesterol.

Weight gain

Cortisol is very similar to the drug cortisone. If you've ever taken cortisone you are aware that it causes you to retain fluid. It also causes your body to gain weight, especially in the tummy and truncal area. That's why those who are dealing with protracted stress often gain weight for seemingly no reason.

Bone loss

Cortisol, much like cortisone, can lead to bone loss. Over the long term, elevation of cortisol may lead to osteopenia and eventually osteoporosis.

Elevated blood pressure

High levels of cortisol for extended periods of

time may elevate your blood pressure by robbing your body of vital minerals such as magnesium, potassium and calcium. Magnesium and potassium are extremely important in maintaining your normal blood pressure.

You already may be aware of how important these minerals are to maintaining strong, healthy bones. Elevated cortisol levels usually cause the body to retain sodium, which may raise your blood pressure. In addition, adrenaline constricts your arteries, with similar results.

Memory loss

Not only does cortisol steal minerals, but it can also bankrupt your body's supply of essential vitamins such as the B vitamins, vitamin C and zinc. B vitamins are really important for maintaining neurotransmitters in your brain for stress control.

Excess cortisol damages the brain by creating excessive amounts of free radicals. These free radicals can eventually destroy brain cells. This destruction of the brain cells leads to memory loss.

Compromised immune system

High cortisol levels over an extended period

of time weaken the immune system. Individuals in the resistance stage of stress also are more prone to bacterial and viral infections, candida and allergies. You may begin to develop allergy symptoms you've never before experienced—sneezing, runny nose, itchy eyes . . . and the list just keeps on going.

Sleep deprivation

Stress also leads to insomnia and sleep disorders. Individuals in the resistance stage or stage 2 are so revved up they often can't sleep well at night. This is usually due to elevated cortisol levels. As you can imagine, without rest stress is increased even more. This downward spiral of stage 2 stress can lead to the third and final stage of stress—*exhaustion.* At this point, you are headed for a crash.

Stage 3—Exhaustion

As your body reaches stage 3 of stress, your downward spiral of stress ends in exhaustion. All of your organs and body systems have been on heightened alert to defend the body from danger for so long that they finally throw up the white flag. Completely spent, you crash and burn. At stage 3, you've usually either run out of gas or are running on fumes—physically, emotionally and spiritually. This is a very dangerous point to reach. Your body has given all it has to give, and now it begins to break down.

When you get to the exhaustion stage, your once robust, powerful body that was designed to remain healthy begins to break down, degenerate and die prematurely. At this final stage of stress, many dramatic changes take place. Let's take a look at some of them.

Immune system depletion

Your immune system that struggled and faltered at stage 2 can now become depleted, opening a Pandora's box. The body is more prone to bacterial and viral infections, allergies, candida and many other illnesses.

As the immune system becomes increasingly depleted, it leads to worsened allergies, environmental illness,

> *For as [a man] thinketh in his heart, so is he.*
> —PROVERBS 23:7, KJV

inflammation of joints, aches and pains, a dramatically reduced resistance to infection and severe fatigue. This state of chronic ill health comes with an emotional and mental fallout. You may become increasingly anxious, irritable and even more depressed. The exhaustion stage of stress may lead to chronic conditions of depression, anxiety and fatigue.

If this process isn't halted, autoimmune diseases such as lupus, rheumatoid arthritis, thyroiditis, multiple sclerosis and eventually even cancer can follow.

Decreased sexual functioning

Your supply of adrenaline and cortisol that has been elevated for so long is used up. Your bank account is now overdrawn. As a result, you now may experience a decrease in sex hormones such as progesterone, testosterone and estrogen, which adversely affects the sexual function.

PMS and perimenopause symptoms

This decrease in sex hormones can have dramatic consequences for women. Progesterone, the raw material for making the stress hormone cortisol, has been depleted also because of living under prolonged stress. When your progesterone is depleted you can develop PMS and symptoms of perimenopause, and you may start menopause much earlier than you would otherwise.

Are You Exhausted?
A Test for Adrenal Exhaustion

If you feel dizzy or lightheaded when you stand up suddenly, it may be an indicator that you are in the exhaustion stage of stress.

A simple screening test for adrenal exhaustion is to have your blood pressure checked while lying down. Rest for five minutes. Then stand up and immediately have your blood pressure checked again. If it drops by ten points, it's very likely that your adrenals are exhausted. Just be sure that you are not dehydrated because that can produce the same effect.

HEALTHFACT HEALTHFACT HEALTHFACT HEALTHFACT HEALTHFACT HEALTHFACT HEALTHFACT

Weight gain

If you've been gaining weight for seemingly no reason, it may indicate that your body is in the exhaustion stage.

The functioning of your thyroid can also be diminished in the exhaustion stage. Remember, during the alarm stage the thyroid responds by increasing the metabolic rate. During stage 3, your adrenals have become exhausted, and thyroid function may also decrease. Therefore, if you are in stage 3, you may have developed a low-functioning thyroid gland, which often is accompanied by a significant weight gain.

At this stage, as we have mentioned, the neurotransmitters in your brain may be imbalanced. Therefore, your serotonin levels may be diminished, which usually causes you to crave sugar and starches.

Low blood sugar

Adrenal exhaustion also may cause the blood sugar to drop. Along with low levels of serotonin, dramatic dips in blood sugar levels also create cravings for sweets and starches.

Because adrenaline and cortisol tend to raise blood sugar, your blood sugar may drop significantly when your reserves of these hormones have been exhausted. You may find yourself needing to eat every couple of hours, or else you feel starved, cranky and irritable.

With the increased calories, you then tend to gain even more weight as you satisfy your craving for more starches, sugars and other carbohydrates. You may even start losing muscle mass as you gain weight. Weight is usually gained in the abdomen, the thighs and the hips.

Very often muscle mass is lost in the arms. What happens to many men is that all of their weight shifts downward. Many get "furniture disease," where their chest shifts down to their "drawers." You've seen men with this disease; they walk around with big bellies that look about nine months pregnant and with skinny little arms and legs. Many such individuals are suffering from the adrenal exhaustion stage of stress. Unaware of this, they may blame their Humpty-Dumpty look on aging.

Digestive problems

As symptoms continue to spiral downward, your stomach can be affected as well. It can begin producing either too much or too little acid. Either of these extremes is harmful and can lead to heartburn, bloating and gas. Too little acid may impair digestion.

This poor fat and protein digestion and absorption can also cause you to lose muscle mass while still gaining fat.

Memory loss

Do you find yourself looking into the face of someone whose name you know but are not able to pull up the information? Prolonged stress impacts your ability to remember things.

The continuous pumping of cortisol into our

bodies actually destroys brain cells. It is like pouring acid on your brain. This degenerative process can eventually lead to memory loss and possibly even Alzheimer's disease. Nevertheless, even a serious state of memory loss can be completely turned around if it's caught in time.

Autoimmune disease

A final stop of this destructive downhill fall may be disease. At this point, instead of the body protecting itself as it has been working very hard to do through stage 1 and stage 2, it may begin attacking itself. That's what autoimmune diseases are all about.

When stress is not dealt with or treated, it can become a violent aggressor, causing your body to destroy itself through autoimmune

> *And the peace I give isn't like the peace the world gives. So don't be troubled or afraid.*
> —JOHN 14:27

diseases such as lupus, rheumatoid arthritis, thyroiditis, Hashimoto's thyroiditis, multiple sclerosis, Type-1 diabetes and many more. Your body has become so run-down that you have opened a door to disaster.

There's Hope for You!

Don't be alarmed if you see yourself in this destructive downward spiral of stress and disease. There is hope for you. Even if your world feels as if it is filled with stress, you have reason to be extremely encouraged.

Jesus Christ said, "In the world ye shall have tribulation: but be of good cheer; I have overcome the world" (John 16:33, KJV). Jesus Christ has the answer for the stressful lives that so many of us feel forced to live.

> *But when the Holy Spirit controls our lives, he will produce this kind of fruit in us: love, joy, peace, patience, kindness, goodness, faithfulness, gentleness, and self-control.*
> —GALATIANS 5:22–23

As you continue to read through this little booklet on stress, you will become increasingly aware that God's plan for you is good health—body, mind and spirit. Better yet, He holds the power over every force in the universe—even your stress. He has answers to your every question and peace for your every fear.

You will conquer stress; it will not conquer you. With God's help, you cannot lose. So, read on and get ready to win the battle!

A BIBLE CURE PRAYER
FOR YOU

Dear Lord Jesus, I thank You that You overcame the entire world through Your death on the cross. Your power is greater than any force in the entire universe—even stress. In fact, You hold the universe. Thank You for putting this little booklet in my hands to show me the way to conquer stress and its dangerous effects in my life. Amen.

A BIBLE CURE PRESCRIPTION

What are your stress-related symptoms?

_____

_____

_____

What level of stress do you believe you may be experiencing? Why?

_____

_____

_____

In your own words thank God for His help in overcoming the dangerous downward spiral of stress.

_____

_____

_____

_____

_____

Chapter 2

Supplement Strategies for Conquering Stress

O ur stressful lifestyles really can feel over-whelming at times. If stress has ever left you feeling defeated and depleted, the Bible has an answer. You see, stress is nothing new. David wrote in the Psalms, "When my heart is over-whelmed: lead me to the rock that is higher than I" (Ps. 61:2, KJV).

In a demanding, turbulent world, it's comfort-ing to remember that Christ is greater than your greatest problem. His tender love is a rock you can stand upon no matter how much the world shakes around you.

You can go to God when you feel overwhelmed and stressed. But what do we do instead? Many of us go to the refrigerator seeking a little "comfort" food to get us through the current round of stress. A slice of pie or a batch of chocolate chip cookies does nothing to reduce your stress. As a matter of fact, as we have seen, sugar can be harmful to an already stressed-out body. It gives a momentary lift, but you've actually further taxed your body and have not dealt with the roots of your stress.

To recover from the sense of burnout, exhaustion and nervous tension of stress, you are going to need to deal with the physical roots that are affecting your emotions and your sense of well-being.

You now realize that stress has wreaked havoc on your physical body and your emotions. Gaining control over stress and its

> *Praise God, who did not ignore my prayer and did not withdraw his unfailing love from me.*
> —PSALM 66:20

unpleasant side effects will involve bringing your physical body back to a healthier state. This can be accomplished through supplements and nutrition.

Supplement Strategies for the Stressed Out

Let's take a look at some supplement solutions that will dramatically impact the way you feel both physically and emotionally.

A comprehensive multivitamin

A good daily multivitamin/multimineral supplement such as Divine Health Multivitamin is essential for building up your body. You can find a good multivitamin at your favorite health food store, or you can find order information for my own Divine Health line of supplements and other products at the back of this booklet.

A comprehensive multivitamin should also contain adequate amounts of B-complex vitamins in the appropriate ratios. B_5, or pantothenic acid, is called the anti-stress vitamin. It plays a significant part in the production of adrenal hormones.

DSF or Cytozyme-AD

DSF, or *De-Stress Formula,* combines glandular supplements, including adrenal glandular and cofactors along with pantothenic acid and other B vitamins to repair and support the adrenal glands.

Cytozyme-AD is an excellent adrenal glandular formula.

Either one of these stress formulas is excellent for both support and repair of the exhausted adrenal glands, which occurs in stage 3 stress. A stress formula is essential if you have been under stress for a prolonged period of time or if you are in the adrenal exhaustion stage of stress.

You can get DSF from Nutri-West by calling 800-874-7318. Take one-half to one tablet swallowed or chewed for better absorption for breakfast and lunch.

Cytozyme-AD can be purchased from Biotics by calling 800-451-5620. Take one to two tablets three times per day.

Green superfood

Take a green food daily to help cleanse your body and boost your immune system. High-chlorophyll foods include wheat grass, barley grass, alfalfa, chlorella, spirulina and blue/green algae. You can purchase Divine Health Green Superfood by calling the number at the back of this booklet. Several other very good chlorophyll supplements can be found on the market as well. These foods are very nutrient-dense and are excellent sources of essential amino acids, vitamins, minerals, essential fatty acids and phytonutrients.

DHEA

DHEA is the most prevalent of the different hormones produced by the adrenal glands. The body actually uses DHEA as the raw material for making the sex hormones testosterone and estrogen. DHEA levels decrease dramatically with age and with excessive amounts of stress over a prolonged period of time. I commonly place men on DHEA if they are in adrenal exhaustion. I then check blood levels for DHEA to insure that they are on the correct dosage.

For men only: Take 25 to 50 milligrams twice a day. Have a checkup and PSA blood test before taking this supplement, however. You should not take this supplement if you have prostate cancer. You can find this supplement at your favorite health food store or by calling the number for Divine Health Nutritional Products at the back of this booklet.

Pregnenolone

Pregnenolone has been called "the grandmother of all steroid hormones" since it's used by the body to make all the steroid hormones. It is also directly linked to your body's supply of DHEA and progesterone. Taking pregnenolone may increase your body's levels of progesterone. Pregnenolone levels decline with age.

Pregnenolone is usually taken in a dose of 50 milligrams once or twice per day. Women in adrenal exhaustion may benefit from taking pregnenolone.

Moducare

Moducare is a supplement that contains plant sterols and sterolins such as Beta-sistosterol. These plants sterols help to regulate the excessive release of cortisol and also to help raise DHEA levels, thus modulating the stress response. This is especially important in Stage 2 or the resistant stage of stress.

I recommend taking two capsules two to three times per day on an empty stomach thirty minutes before meals. You can order these supplements by contacting Divine Health Nutritional Products at the back of this book.

Phosphatidyl serine

Phosphatidyl serine is derived from soybeans, and it has been used primarily for its cognitive effects. It appears to help preserve and even improve memory in a dose of 300 milligrams per day.

However, phosphatidyl serine and other phosphatides also have cortisol suppressive properties. This supplement will help lower cortisol levels after intense exercise as well as reduce excess cortisol production during sleep. That's important if you're in Stage 2 or the resistance stage of stress.

I recommend the supplement Pro-Cortisol

Balance, which is available from Nutri-West at 800-451-5620. The dose is usually two to three tablets after exercise, exertion or stress, and two to three tablets again in the evening at bedtime.

Ginseng

Interestingly, there are three different herbs that are all called ginseng. They are Korean or Asian (panax) ginseng, Siberian ginseng and American ginseng.

Ginseng is an adaptogen that helps the body adapt to both physical and psychological stress. Nevertheless, no scientific evidence exists at present to support this notion.

> *May God our Father give you grace and peace.*
> —COLOSSIANS 1:2

Korean ginseng tends to be the most effective variety of the three. A typical dosage is 100 to 200 milligrams of standardized extract that supplies 4 to 7 percent ginsenosides.

Ginseng may be helpful in both Stage 2 and Stage 3 of stress.

Find out about other herbs and supplements that may also be effective for relieving stress by referring to *The Bible Cure for Depression and Anxiety.*

Natural progesterone cream

For women in the perimenopause or menopause years, a natural progesterone cream is essential if you're battling stress, especially if your body is in Stage 3 or the exhaustion stage of stress.

In fact, many pre-menopausal women are low in progesterone, even though they continue to have

> *Let this mind be in you, which was also in Christ Jesus.*
> —PHILIPPIANS 2:5, KJV

normal periods, especially if they are under considerable, long-term stress.

A simple blood test checking the level of progesterone will determine if you are low or borderline low.

I place women on a natural progesterone cream (3 percent) called Natural Change Cream from Nutri-West. Apply ¼ teaspoon two times a day. Contact Nutri-West at 800-451-5620.

A Rule of Thumb

Here's a list of the supplements you may take to strengthen and support your body as it deals with the challenge of stress.

Supplements for Stage 2

- A comprehensive multivitamin (such as Divine Health Multivitamin)
- Green Superfood
- Moducare
- Procortisol Balance

Supplements for Stage 3 for men

- A comprehensive multivitamin
- Green Superfood
- DHEA
- DSF or Cytozme AD
- Moducare

Supplements for Stage 3 for women

- A comprehensive multivitamin
- Green Superfood
- Pregnenolone
- Natural progesterone cream
- DSF or Cytozyme AD
- Moducare

Ginseng can be added to your supplement list for both men and women at stages 2 and 3.

In Conclusion

You don't have to let stress rob you of your strength, energy, vitality, happiness and joy. You can take back your health by rebuilding your body through powerful supplements. You will feel refreshed, restored and reinvigorated in no time.

A BIBLE CURE PRAYER FOR YOU

Dear Lord, thank You for providing natural solutions to restore my health. Grant me the wisdom I need to select the proper supplements. I thank You for restoring my joy, energy, happiness and peace. In Jesus' name, amen.

A BIBLE CURE PRESCRIPTION

List the supplements you are planning to take to help your body combat stress.

_____

_____

_____

_____

_____

_____

Write a prayer thanking God for your complete recovery from the negative effects of stress in your life.

_____

_____

_____

_____

_____

Chapter 3

Exercise Strategies for Conquering Stress

God wants to bless you with the peaceful joy of a stress-free life. As a matter of fact, God promises to strengthen your body and to give peace to your mind and soul. The Bible says, "The LORD will give strength to His people; the LORD will bless His people with peace" (Ps. 29:11, NKJV).

A powerful strategy for conquering stress is exercise. Exercise provides an extremely beneficial avenue for releasing pent-up stress and negative emotions. Instead of allowing stress to tear down your body, you can actually use stress to an advantage.

A good workout can dissipate stress and leave you feeling great. Let's look at some exercises you can do to conquer stress so that it never conquers you, including some relaxation exercises that will help you to unwind.

Three-Minute Relaxation Routine

This relaxation routine takes only three minutes, but it can be a lifesaver in a tense situation.

1. Concentrate on relaxing using a cue word, such as *God's peace* or *God's love.* Listen to your own breathing, and take in one deep breath and hold it in.
2. While you are holding your breath, tense up a group of muscles, such as the muscles in your face, legs or arms.
3. As you release the breath, relax the tense muscle group. Feel all your tension slip away. Drop your shoulders down and rotate them in a circle.
4. Repeat.

You can do this relaxation exercise while you're at work or at home. Learning to relax takes practice. Relaxation training reduces anxiety and stress, and it decreases heart disease and high blood pressure.[1]

Progressive Muscle Relaxation

In this relaxation exercise, you must tighten each muscle group in your body, hold it for five seconds, and then gradually release the muscles and relax them for ten to fifteen minutes. Relaxing your entire body through this technique will take about twenty minutes.

1. Sit or lie down quietly in a comfortable position away from noise or distractions.
2. Scan your body to identify areas of stress or tension.
3. Begin to tense and tighten your muscles in each of the following muscle groups, beginning at your head. Tense each body part for five seconds, and then slowly release the tension as you focus on the body part. This needs to be repeated twice for each muscle group. As you learn to slowly release the tension in your muscles, you will actually be teaching your body how to relax.

- Forehead and top of head—raise eyebrows
- Jaw—clench teeth
- Neck—pull chin forward onto your chest
- Shoulders and trapezoid muscles—lift shoulders
- Back—pull back shoulder blades
- Arms—flex biceps
- Abdomen—tighten abdomen
- Buttocks—squeeze and tighten buttocks
- Thighs—flex thighs
- Calves—flex and point toes up or down[2]

A BIBLE CURE HEALTH TIP

Melt Away Stress

Essential oils can be added directly to your bath water. Here's how:

- Add 5–10 drops of essential oils to hot water while filling your bath.

- Do not combine essential oils with other bath oils or soap.

- Make sure to soak in the tub for at least twenty minutes to get the aromatic benefits.

You can find essential oils at health food stores.

The following essential oils have properties that are especially beneficial.

Lavender. At first this oil may pep you up a little. But as you soak for a few minutes, you'll find that it calms you. It relieves nervous tension, depression and insomnia.

Geranium. Combine a couple drops of this with lavender. It has a calming effect.

Rosemary. This one helps circulation. Use it alone or with lavender to relieve depression.

Baking Soda or Epson Salt. A hot bath in baking soda can do wonders for relaxing your muscles. Scoop a handful of baking soda or 1–2 cups of epson salt into very hot bath water and relax.

Get Hooked on Regular Exercise

Regular aerobic exercise doesn't have to be a chore. As a matter of fact, it can be a lot of fun. Instead of always getting together with your friends for lunch or dessert, why not try meeting your friends for a walk or tennis?

Brisk walking or bicycling are great ways to get in shape and release stress. What about joining a square dancing club or taking ballroom dancing lessons? I guarantee you'll wonder why you didn't try it sooner.

A Simple Walking Program

(NOTE: Each column indicates the number of minutes to walk. Complete three exercise sessions each week. If you find a particular week's pattern tiring, repeat it before going on to the next pattern. You do not have to complete the walking program in twelve weeks.)

Week	—Walk	—Walk Briskly	—Walk	—Minutes
1	5	5	5	15
2	5	7	5	17
3	5	9	5	19
4	5	11	5	21
5	5	13	5	23
6	5	15	5	25
7	5	18	5	28
8	5	20	5	30
9	5	23	5	33
10	5	26	5	36
11	5	28	5	38
12	5	30	5	40

Week 13 and thereafter: Check your pulse periodically to see if you are exercising within your target zone. As you get more in shape, try exercising within the upper range of your target zone. Gradually increase your brisk walking time from 30 to 60 minutes, three or four times a week. Remember that your goal is to get the benefits you are seeking and enjoy your activity.

Use the following chart to determine your target heart rate zone while exercising. Once you have determined your desired range, stay within it.

A BIBLE CURE HEALTH TIP

Your Target Heart Rate Zone

Calculate your target heart rate zone using this formula:

220 minus [your age] = _____
x .65 = _____
[This is your minimum.]

220 minus [your age] = _____
x .80 = _____
[This is your maximum.]

This example may help: To calculate the target heart zone for a 40-year-old man, subtract the age (40) from 220 (220- 40=180). Multiply 180 by .65, which equals 117. Then multiply 180 by .80, which equals 144. A 40-year-old man's target heart rate zone is 117–144 beats per minute.

Regular exercise improves heart health, lung function, circulation and blood pressure. It reduces fat and lowers cholesterol. Regular exercise relaxes your muscles, reduces stress and decreases fatigue. As you exercise, your body also releases endorphins, which are natural antidepressants and pain relievers that make you feel better.

So, to boost your self-image, build your confidence and increase your energy, determine to start exercising twenty minutes a day for at least three days per week.

A word of caution: If you feel you are in the exhaustion stage of stress, wait a few months until you build

> *For thus saith the LORD, Behold, I will extend peace to her like a river.*
> —ISAIAH 66:12, KJV

up your body with adequate nutrition and rest before getting into an aerobic exercise program.

In Conclusion

The apostle Paul said, "But I discipline my body and bring it into subjection, lest, when I have preached to others, I myself should become disqualified" (1 Cor. 9:27, NKJV). Paul's life was filled with stressful situations. Still, he took charge over his body through discipline. In that way he avoided being defeated by the effects of stress.

What about you? Why not choose to conquer stress and its devastating effects on your body?

Why not make up your mind right now to include regular exercise in your lifestyle choices? Exercise can make a stressful period of life more bearable. It can make a lifestyle of stress endurable. Exercise can give you the strength you need to go the distance.

A BIBLE CURE PRAYER FOR YOU

Dear Lord, give me the discipline and motivation I need to invest faithfully in a regular program of exercise to help me manage stress. Thank You for Your promise to strengthen me—body, mind and spirit. Amen.

Write out your plan for a regular exercise program that includes stress management techniques.

_____

_____

_____

_____

_____

Write a prayer in your own words asking God for His help to keep you at it.

_____

_____

_____

_____

_____

Chapter 4

Mental Strategies for Conquering Stress

Believe it or not, you can live a life that is free of the negative effects of stress. God actually promises a way to have a peaceful, happy mind no matter how stressful your circumstances. The prophet declared to God, "You will keep him in perfect peace, whose mind is stayed on You, because he trusts in You" (Isa. 26:3, NKJV).

The Bible provides a strategy for living free from the negative effects associated with stress. You can live in God's wonderful peace every day of your life no matter what disappointments you face, what pressures you must endure and no matter how many difficult, stressful circumstances surround your life.

It almost sounds too good to be true, but it's not.

Let's take a look at some strategies from the Bible that promise peace—no matter what!

Renewing Your Mind

We have mentioned that not everyone experiences the same stress reactions to the same life events. For one person, speaking in front of a large group feels like a fun challenge, but it makes another individual a nervous wreck. If one person's relaxation is another person's stress, then circumstances are not the sole cause of stress. Your individual perception of the events in your life plays a vital role in your experience of stress as well.

Therefore, a powerful strategy for conquering stress is to deal with the roots of stress in your own life by beginning to change your own perceptions and reactions to circumstances. This powerful strategy is taken directly from the Bible. The apostle Paul declared:

> Don't copy the behavior and customs of this world, but let God transform you into a new person by changing the way you think. Then you will know what God wants you to do, and you will know how good and pleasing and perfect his will really is.
> —ROMANS 12:2

With God's help, we can develop new, less stressful ways of thinking. Doing so, in fact, is a command from God's Word. It says, "Be renewed in the spirit of your mind" (Eph. 4:23, NKJV).

Renewing the mind is nothing more than breaking the thought patterns and ways of thinking and perceiving life's circumstances that cause us stress. I call these stressful patterns "stinking thinking." Let's take a look at some successful strategies for renewing the mind by breaking the power of stressful stinking thinking.

Overcoming Stinking Thinking

We all encounter stressful circumstances throughout our days, but to overcome the roots of stress we must address how we believe, perceive and react to that stress.

Your ability to cope with stress may be rooted in your personality. Most of us fall into one of three personality categories. They are:

- Passive
- Aggressive
- Assertive

If you are passive, you may have difficulty expressing your thoughts and feelings. You also find it difficult to stand up for yourself. Others tend to walk all over you, and they are able to influence you and even to make decisions for you. Passive people are usually always apologizing. They maintain poor eye contact, looking away or down to the floor when you talk with them.

Passive Personalities

Many of our parents believed, "Spare the rod, spoil the child." They tried to instill healthy values in us by dominating, criticizing and controlling us. Some parents beat us into submission verbally, and some did so physically. When your six-foot-tall father hovered over your two-and-a-half-foot frame, holding a whipping belt in his hand, what did you say? "I give! I give! I will do anything you say."

Unfortunately, many individuals who are raised with this kind of heavy-handed, "over-discipline" approach never grow into assertive adults. As children they submit to over-discipline, and then they stay submitted throughout life. They remain passive like a doormat. People walk all over them, or they are easily taken advantage of, easily controlled and easily led.

This is only one reason folks become passive; there are others.

Express Yourself

Passive people are unable to adequately express their thoughts and feelings and usually are not able to stand up for themselves. Passive individuals seek out others who will do battle for them. They may share their anger or hostility with a person and expect that person to vindicate their cause. In this way passivity can lead to manipulative behaviors, which are also destructive to relationships.

If you recognize yourself as a passive personality type, God wants to set you free. He wants to teach you to express yourself and to be more assertive in Him.

One reason people get stuck in this non-assertive, passive lifestyle is their fear of rejection. They have good hearts and good motives, but they let the fear of rejection control their lives. Rather than assert their feelings or ideas and risk not being accepted, they settle for passivity.

Aggressive Personalities

Under an iron-fisted child-rearing approach, some kids flip and go the other way. Instead of becoming passive, they may become extremely aggressive. Rejecting parental authority, they determine that they won't be bullied anymore, and they may become the bullies. Other youngsters who receive too little discipline can often go this route as well. These children are usually defiant and rebellious, and they usually grow up to become pushy, dominating and intimidating adults.

Aggressive behavior dominates, intimidates or bullies others. It is very confrontational. These people may get in your face and point their finger at you. They tend to view their

> *So don't get tired of doing what is good. Don't get discouraged and give up, for we will reap a harvest of blessing at the appropriate time.*
> —GALATIANS 6:9

own needs as priority and may stop at nothing to get what they want, including belittling, shouting, deliberately hurting and bullying others.

You've encountered aggressive people on the highways. The aggressive drivers will look directly in your face as they stare you down. They may glare at you, cross their arms, point or clench their fists.

Aggressive personalities can thrive in the corporate business environment. They enjoy hostile takeovers: one corporate giant takes over another's business or one secretary rises above her peers by campaigning against everyone she considers a threat. Aggressive personalities will usually walk all over others to get to the top.

Passive/Aggressive People

The personality type of some individuals is a little more difficult to recognize. These folks are actually very aggressive, but they appear passive at first glance. We could call them passive/aggressive personalities. They seem to submit and yield easily to others, but inwardly they seldom do so. They maintain a steel core of resistance inside that they express in nonaggressive ways. Instead of confronting a rival, a passive/aggressive individual will find subtle ways to "get him" behind his back, including backbiting, gossip, slander, lies and more. These stealthy souls can be particularly treacherous. Another version of this personality can be very confusing because it will indicate one intention but actually do the opposite.

Those who relate to passive/aggressive people eventually feel betrayed by them, because passive/aggressive people seem to present their motives in one way when their true feelings are often quite different. It may not be deliberate, for often passive/aggressive people are seldom in touch with their own true feelings. In a sense, they betray themselves together with everyone around them.

The Assertive Personality

God designed us to be raised in families surrounded by lots of love, encouragement and freedom to express ourselves so that our personalities could develop and grow into healthy assertiveness.

God wants you to be assertive in Him, not passive or aggressive. Assertiveness allows you to communicate clearly, confidently and boldly your thoughts, feelings, wants and

> *But the wisdom that comes from heaven is first of all pure. It is also peace loving, gentle at all times, and willing to yield to others.*
> —JAMES 3:17

desires. Assertiveness is developed in a loving, stable home environment where there is lots of encouragement, freedom to express yourself, healthy structure and discipline, support and acceptance.

Assertive children have a healthy and strong sense of identity. Children learn assertiveness through healthy, strong, loving relationships with parents, siblings, teachers, friends and neighbors.

Sadly, many of our lives fall short of God's design. Think back to your own experiences. Were you raised with lots of praise and encouragement? Or did your parents tell you, "You are not going to amount to anything. You are worthless, hopeless and helpless. You can't do anything right."

As a result, guess what? From childhood many were programmed for failure. The roots of our stress can be the tapes that play over and over in our subconscious minds, saying, "I am not good enough." "I'm a loser." "I'm bad." "I'm hopeless." "There's no hope for me." "I'm unloved." "I'm rejected." "I'm a failure."

Even if you did not grow up learning how to be assertive, you're not stuck with a stress-producing personality

> *Casting all your care upon Him, for He cares for you.*
> —1 PETER 5:7, NKJV

style. You can learn assertiveness by renewing your mind with some new skills. Here are some tips to get started:

- Begin communicating your thoughts, feelings, wants and needs more confidently.
- Learn to say no.
- Respect other people and their rights.
- Don't let other people walk all over you.

- Don't respond to others apologetically.
- Avoid aggression, and never put others down or walk over them.

Let's look at some of these strategies for renewing the mind by overcoming some common types of stinking thinking that can create unnecessary stress in your life and relationships.

Just Say No

A major characteristic of an assertive individual is the power to say no, unapologetically, gently, respectfully and kindly.

You might be surprised at how difficult that can be for most of us. Learning to say no is one of the most important things you can do—and it is one of the best tools for developing assertiveness.

There's always someone who wants to borrow your car, your clothes, your money, your lawn mower or who wants to fill up your days with their own chores and responsibilities. When you are unable to say no to a person's request, that person's problem has now become your problem, and his or her burden is now your burden.

Instead of churning in emotional circles of frustration and anger, simply say, "No, I can't. Send my greetings to everyone at home."

No apologizing, no long explanations—just simply, politely say no and move on to another topic.

Boiling Over

Remember the children's song "I'm a Little Teapot"? It goes, "When I get all steamed up, hear me shout." Passive people can be just like that teapot. They can wait until their frustrations rise to a boiling point, and then they spill over with hot anger and pent-up frustrations, saying hurtful things they've left unsaid for months and even years.

This kind of emotional release is often very destructive to friendships and everyone's self-esteem, especially the passive person's.

Learning to say no in a polite, respectful, unapologetic way will build your confidence and self-esteem. Keep in mind that you are not rejecting the person making the request; you are merely rejecting the request. Your kind, loving attitude will project that truth.

Communicating Assertively

Another powerful strategy to help you become more assertive is learning to communicate your thoughts, feelings, wants and needs confidently.

A BIBLE CURE HEALTH TIP

Here are some tips for communicating assertively:

- Don't look down while talking.
- Maintain eye contact without staring down the other person.
- Don't cross your arms.
- Don't clench your fists.
- Don't point your fingers.
- Stand or sit erect but relaxed.
- Keep your hands open.
- Don't look haggard, beaten down or defeated with hunched shoulders.
- Speak boldly and firmly, but lovingly and respectfully.
- Never shout.
- Never sound sarcastic.
- Never intimidate.

Boosting Your Own Self Esteem

By learning assertiveness you can strengthen your self-confidence and improve your self-image. Jesus was the prime example of self-confidence.

He was more kind and loving than any person who ever walked the earth, and yet He boldly spoke the truth without timidity.

He wants us to have a strong self-identity and high self-esteem. We are supposed to love ourselves. He told us to "love your neighbor as yourself" (Matt. 19:19). We must love ourselves, not in a selfish, self-indulgent way, but with a healthy sense of self-worth and self esteem.

> *He rebuked the wind and said to the water, "Quiet down!" Suddenly the wind stopped, and there was a great calm.*
> —MARK 4:39

Too many of us hate ourselves, and as a result, we hate our bodies. Women develop a sense of how they should look by reading women's magazines that feature anorexic models. By comparing themselves to other women, they develop a deep dissatisfaction with their looks.

Reject Rigid Words

Are you plagued with thoughts that sound like this:

- "I should have done that."
- "I have to go there."
- "I should have been there."

- "I must do that."

These rigid words can reveal another type of stinking thinking:

- Should
- Must
- Have to
- Ought to
- Expected to
- Can't

Such words are rigid and don't allow for much flexibility in your thinking. Such thinking leads to frustration, guilt, shame, blame, anger and depression. Let your words, even your mental words, be seasoned with God's grace. Root out rigid words and replace them with grace words such as:

- May
- With the Lord's help
- Can

You Really Can Change

If you have stinking thinking, you continually say to

yourself, "I cannot change. I'll always be this way."

If you have heard yourself express such sentiments, then you too may be a stinking thinker. You can always change with God's help, for He promises to change us for the better.

The Bible says, "But we all, with open face beholding as in a glass the glory of the Lord, are changed into the same image form glory to glory, even as by the Spirit of the Lord" (2 Cor. 3:17–18, KJV).

Under the Circumstances . . .

Get out from under the circumstances! You cannot control all of the circumstances around you, but you can control how you respond. Circumstances can change in your life just as easily as the direction of the wind. If your happiness is based upon your circumstances, you will be up one day and down the next.

James 1:2–4 says, "My brethren, count it all joy when you fall into various trials, knowing that the testing of your faith produces patience. But let patience have its perfect work, that you may be perfect and complete, lacking nothing" (NKJV).

Force yourself to look for the good in every situation. Depending upon your personality, this can be easier for some than others. Nevertheless, you can make the choice to be thankful for the good things you do have, even when your circumstances are extremely taxing. Seek to find some redemptive purpose in everything that happens. As you train your mind to find the positive, you may discover that the negative circumstances in your life—difficult as they are—no longer feel so overwhelming.

Reject Perfectionism and Unrealistic Expectations

It is unrealistic for you to expect yourself to be perfect. The only perfect person was Jesus Christ. Perfectionism can cause you to become critical of yourself and everyone else around you. Perfectionists place themselves under enormous amounts of unnecessary stress. God has not placed impossible demands on you. He isn't looking for perfect people; He's looking for people who are willing to be yielded vessels. Here's what His Word says:

> And what does the LORD require of you but to do justly, to love mercy, and to walk humbly with your God?
>
> —MICAH 6:8, NKJV

These are merely a few major types of stinking thinking that rob our lives through dangerous stress. There are many; you may be able to think of several others yourself. Renewing your mind with principles from God's Word will help you overcome these negative, stressful approaches to your life.

Practice Time Management

Learning new ways of managing your time can dramatically reduce your stress as well. If you are forty years old, statistically you have used up more than half of your life on this earth. Have you ever stopped to reflect on how wise you've been in the management of that time? Learning to manage your time is critically important for conquering stress. Let's take a look at a few extremely important time management strategies.

Avoid time suckers

Do you know what a "sucker" is? Farmers know that trees must be pruned to cut off the suckers. These are large branches that grow out of control and tend to sap the tree of all of its energy and nourishment. When the farmer prunes his apple trees or pear trees, he cuts off those branches so the entire tree can be nourished in a balanced, healthy way.

This phenomenon also occurs in our lives with our time. We all experience time suckers. These are activities, relationships, business ventures and anything else that robs our lives of enormous amounts of time and energy to the point at which the overall health of our lives is depleted. Suckers drain us and pull us off of the path of health and godliness.

A sucker can be as simple as the onslaught of telemarketing calls you receive each evening at dinner time that steals away your

> *The LORD gives his people strength. The LORD blesses them with peace.*
> —PSALM 29:11

peaceful family moments. Or a sucker can be as major as a close relationship with a relative who is controlling and overbearing and who is stealing your family's harmony in order to meet his or her own needs through you.

One of the most important things you can do is to identify the time suckers in your life and take steps to eliminate or reduce their negative effect.

Plan your work, and work your plan

Highly successful people will tell you that one of the most important keys to success is planning.

The Bible says, "Where there is no vision, the people perish" (Prov. 29:18, KJV).

Have you prayerfully set goals for your life? Have you prayerfully created a plan for your business or ministry? Do you have a vision for exercise, diet and health? Have you prayerfully developed a plan for reaching the objectives you feel are important? Careful, wise and prayerful planning plays a vital role in reducing stress and helping you reach your objectives.

What is your purpose? Proverbs 19:21 says, "You can make many plans, but the LORD's purpose will prevail." Pray to know God's purpose for you. Start by following your passion!

Learn to delegate

I run a hectic medical practice, so occasionally I have a massage therapist come to our busy office to give a few of the staff a massage, which is also a great stress reliever. Often the massage therapist remarks how relaxed and unstressed my muscles are compared to others on staff whose muscles are knotted from stress. I believe this is because I've learned to delegate effectively, which allows me to accomplish a great deal without becoming overly stressed.

Learn to delegate; you don't have to do it all. If

you don't have a good reason for doing a certain job or duty, then delegate it so that you will have time to do the things you enjoy.

Do It Now!

Did you know that those who procrastinate often have a fear of rejection or failure, which causes them to put off accomplishing certain tasks? Determine that with God's help you will confront your fears, roll up your sleeves and get busy.

Create a plan for accomplishing your tasks, and then slowly start chipping away at them one piece at a time. Once you have completed a particular job, reward yourself for a job well done.

All Work and No Play

Be sure your life has a healthy balance of work and play, difficult jobs and easy ones, tasks you enjoy and those you consider drudgery. All work and no play is unhealthy and will cause you to feel stressed out. If you work very hard, make sure you take vacations and short getaways. Balance is a key factor in health and happiness.

Clean Off Your Plate

One reason you may be feeling overly stressed is

because you have too much on your plate. You may have more debts, commitments, responsibilities and demands than you are able to handle. If you are overextended, clear your plate.

Pay off your debts. Most of us can't do that all at once, but setting a plan in place to do so will eliminate a mountain of stress.

Stop volunteering for duties that you don't have time for. You have a right to save some time for you. Don't get involved in more volunteer, school, church or work activities or projects than you can easily and effectively handle. If you are feeling stressed out, back off a little until your life feels more in control.

Conclusion

Don't let a mountain of stress avalanche down upon your life and health. There's so much you can do to conquer that mountain and rise to the top. God never intended for stress to rob your life of happiness and peace.

Why not determine right now to begin implementing these mental strategies for conquering stress. Living stressed out is not God's best for you. His wonderful Word says:

Don't worry about anything; instead,

70

pray about everything. Tell God what you need and thank him for all he has done. If you do this, you will experience God's peace, which is far more wonderful than the human mind can understand. His peace will guard your hearts and minds as you live in Christ Jesus.

—PHILIPPIANS 4:6–7

With God's help and some wise strategies, you can develop entirely new, stress-free ways of living your life.

A BIBLE CURE PRAYER FOR YOU

Dear Lord, I give You all of my stress-producing ways of thinking and living. Renew my mind by helping me to develop and learn new lifestyle strategies so that I may enjoy greater productivity, happiness and peace. In Jesus' name, amen.

A BIBLE CURE PRESCRIPTION

List all the things you must do.

_____

_____

List all the things you want to do.

_____

_____

List the things you currently do that you neither want to do or must do.

_____

_____

Draw a giant X over the items in list three. These are the things you need to eliminate from your life in order to deal with stress. Develop a plan to eliminate or reduce all of these items in six months. Write out that plan.

_____

_____

_____

Chapter 5

Spiritual Strategies for Conquering Stress

You can begin to manage stress by developing a new belief system that sees God as the One who is in control of your life. The Bible says, "Seek ye first the kingdom of God, and his righteousness; and all these things will be added unto you" (Matt. 6:33, KJV). God will add to your life the peace, happiness and control that you need when you give Him first place.

How do you do this? You must abide in the vine. In other words, you must learn to see Jesus Christ as the complete and total source of your life. When you do so, you will be walking in the Spirit. Galatians 5:16–17 (NIV) says:

> So I say, live by the Spirit, and you will not gratify the desires of the sinful

nature. For the sinful nature desires what is contrary to the Spirit, and the Spirit what is contrary to the sinful nature. They are in conflict with each other, so that you do not do what you want.

Your mind acts like a referee choosing how you will receive and perceive the events of your life. Will you feel overwhelmed by them, or confident and in control no matter what happens? If you get your mind on the side of the Spirit by filling it with God's Word, you will rise above every negative, harmful and stress-producing emotion.

Removing the Roots of Stress

The Word of God is very powerful. It has the power to reprogram the way you think, causing your thinking to line up with God's way of seeing things. When you renew your mind with God's Word, you begin to pull out stressful ways of thinking by their very roots. The Bible says, "We take captive every thought to make it obedient to Christ" (2 Cor. 10:5, NIV).

When my patients come to me with physical and emotional symptoms that are rooted in stress, I prescribe scriptures to help them renew their minds along with a prescription to strengthen their bodies. Here's how it works.

If your mind tells you: "You'll never amount to anything," you can reprogram your mind with God's Word by responding as follows:

> God tells me in Deuteronomy 28:13, "The Lord will make me the head, not the tail. If I pay attention to the commands of the Lord my God and follow them, I will always be at the top and never at the bottom."

At the end of this chapter, I have prepared a Bible Cure prescription for you with God's Word that is specifically directed at your own personal roots of stress, your own stinking thinking. Whenever you hear your own mind speak negative, stress-producing thoughts, you can reprogram it with these verses provided to yank your stress up by the roots.

In addition, here are some more keys to renewing the mind with God's Word.

Practice Forgiveness

Many people harbor hidden anger, bitterness, unforgiveness, resentment, fear, hatred, abandonment, shame and rejection, and aren't even aware of it. What about you? Do memories of old wounds and hurts surface in your thoughts when you encounter certain people? Have you been hurt in the past and simply buried the hurt? Feelings buried alive never die.

Holding on to unforgiveness doesn't punish the individual who wronged you. It only destroys you

> *I am leaving you with a gift—peace of mind and heart.*
> —JOHN 14:27

through the roots of stress. Mark 11:25–26 says, "And when you stand praying, if you hold anything against anyone, forgive him, so that your Father in heaven may forgive your sins" (NIV).

Divine Forgetfulness

Not only do you need to forgive those who have hurt and offended you, but you also need to forget it. "Forgetting what is behind and straining toward what is ahead, I press on toward the goal to win the prize for which God has called me heavenward in Christ Jesus" (Phil. 3:13–14, NIV).

Learn to Love

First Corinthians 13:8 says, "Love never fails" (NKJV). Are you in a political battle at work? Do you have strife in your family? Have you been hurt by your spouse? Love truly never fails—and it will not fail you!

Fear rules the lives of many people. The Bible says, "Perfect love expels fear" (1 John 4:18). You can live free from fear as you increasingly understand the power of God's love for you. Mahatma Gandhi said that the whole world would accept the Christ of Christians if the Christians would only act like Christ.

Build and maintain the ties of relationships. Relationships with those who love you are gifts from God. Never take them for granted!

Learn to Laugh

The Bible says, "A cheerful heart is good medicine" (Prov. 17:22). If you are stressed out, why not take a prescription for laughter? When you're down or stressed, pick up a wholesome funny video and watch it. A good belly laugh can actually massage your internal organs. Author Norman Cousins actually used the healing power of laughter to help him overcome a serious disease.

Laughter releases tension, anxiety, anger, fear, shame and guilt, and it can transform your attitude and outlook.

Keys to Spiritual Health

Here are some keys that can open the doors to a fresh outlook, a new attitude and brand-new you!

- Be born again.
- Renew your mind.
- Watch your thoughts and words.
- Laugh.
- Forgive.
- Maintain relationships and walk in love.

A Bible Cure Prayer
FOR YOU

Dear heavenly Father, I boldly come before Your throne asking for Your power for a brand-new mind, completely transformed by Your mighty and wonderful Word. I submit my life to You, and I ask You to change the way I think and feel. Let my mind line up with the ways that You think. Let my heart rise up in new faith and love. Restore and heal my body from the ravages of stress. Strengthen and renew me completely so that I can walk in Your light and extend Your love to a stressed-out, weary world. In Jesus' name, amen.

A BIBLE CURE PRESCRIPTION

Below you will find some negative thoughts and scriptures that directly uproot those stressful thoughts. Select the verses that are most appropriate to you, and write them down on index cards. Speak them aloud three times a day, at breakfast, lunch and bedtime.

"I'm a failure and a loser."—Romans 8:37; Philippians 4:13

"I'm worthless and pitiful."—2 Corinthians 6:16; Galatians 4:7; Ephesians 2:10

"I'm no good."—2 Corinthians 5:17

"I'm stupid and dumb."—1 Corinthians 1:30; 2:16; James 1:5

"I'm unattractive."—1 Samuel 16:7; Romans 5:5; Ephesians 2:10

"I'm not teachable."—Psalm 32:8

"I'm a burden."—Deuteronomy 28:8

"I'm trapped."—John 8:32, 36

"I'm alone."—Matthew 28:20; Hebrews 13:5

"I'm guilty."—Psalm 103:12; John 1:9; Romans 8:1

"I'm incapable."—Philippians 4:13

"I'm sinful."—John 3:14–18; 5:24

A PERSONAL NOTE

From Don and Mary Colbert

God desires to heal you of disease. His Word is full of promises that confirm His love for you and His desire to give you His abundant life. His desire includes more than physical health for you; He wants to make you whole in your mind and spirit as well through a personal relationship with His Son, Jesus Christ.

If you haven't met my best friend, Jesus, I would like to take this opportunity to introduce Him to you. It is very simple.

If you are ready to let Him come into your heart and become your best friend, just bow your head and sincerely pray this prayer from your heart:

Lord Jesus, I want to know You as my Savior and Lord. I believe You are the Son of God and that You died for my sins. I also believe You were raised from the dead and now sit at the right hand of the Father praying for me. I ask You to forgive me for my sins and change my heart so that I can be Your child and live with You eternally.

Thank You for Your peace. Help me to walk with You so that I can begin to know You as my best friend and my Lord. Amen.

If you have prayed this prayer, we rejoice with you in your decision and your new relationship with Jesus. Please contact us at pray4me@strang.com so that we can send you some materials that will help you become established in your relationship with the Lord. You have just made the most important decision of your life. We look forward to hearing from you.

Notes

PREFACE

FEELING STRESSED OUT?

1. Source obtained from the Internet: http://www.stress.org/problem.htm, 4/30/01.

CHAPTER 3

EXERCISE STRATEGIES FOR CONQUERING STRESS

1. Trevor Powell, *Free Yourself From Harmful Stress* (New York: DJ Publishing, 1997), 128.
2. Ibid., 129.

Don Colbert, M.D., was born in Tupelo, Mississippi. He attended Oral Roberts School of Medicine in Tulsa, Oklahoma, where he received a bachelor of science degree in biology in addition to his degree in medicine. Dr. Colbert completed his internship and residency with Florida Hospital in Orlando, Florida. He is board certified in family practice and has received extensive training in nutritional medicine.

If you would like more
information about natural and
divine healing, or information about
Divine Health Nutritional Products®,
you may contact
Dr. Colbert at:

DR. DON COLBERT

1908 Boothe Circle
Longwood, FL 32750
Telephone: 407-331-7007
(For ordering products only)

Dr. Colbert's website is
www.drcolbert.com.

Disclaimer: Dr. Colbert and the staff of Divine Health Wellness Center are prohibited from addressing a patient's medical condition by phone, facsimile or e-mail. Please refer questions related to your medical condition to your own primary care physician.

Pick up these other Siloam Press
books by Dr. Colbert:

Toxic Relief
Walking in Divine Health
What You Don't Know May Be Killing You

The Bible Cure® Booklet Series

The Bible Cure for ADD and Hyperactivity
The Bible Cure for Allergies
The Bible Cure for Arthritis
The Bible Cure for Back Pain
The Bible Cure for Cancer
The Bible Cure for Candida and Yeast Infection
The Bible Cure for Chronic Fatigue and Fibromyalgia
The Bible Cure for Depression and Anxiety
The Bible Cure for Diabetes
The Bible Cure for Headaches
The Bible Cure for Heart Disease
The Bible Cure for Heartburn and Indigestion
The Bible Cure for Hepatitis and Hepatitis C
The Bible Cure for High Blood Pressure
The Bible Cure for Irritable Bowel Syndrome
The Bible Cure for Memory Loss
The Bible Cure for Menopause
The Bible Cure for Osteoporosis
The Bible Cure for PMS and Mood Swings
The Bible Cure for Prostate Disorders
The Bible Cure for Skin Disorders
The Bible Cure for Sleep Disorders
The Bible Cure for Stress
The Bible Cure for Weight Loss and Muscle Gain

SILOAM PRESS

A part of Strang Communications Company
600 Rinehart Road
Lake Mary, FL 32746
(800) 599-5750